SEO

SIMPLIFIED

LEARN SEARCH ENGINE OPTIMIZATION STRATEGIES AND PRINCIPLES FOR BEGINNERS

R.L. Adams

R.L. ADAMS

All Rights Reserved

FTC & Legal Notices

R.L. ADAMS

CONTENTS

WHAT IS SEO?

SEO is search engine optimization. It is the way that you go about fine-tuning a Webpage to increase its visibility on search engines like Google. I have been professionally involved in SEO for over 10 years now, but my experience with it dates back to the dawn of the Web, before Google was even born.

Many people look at SEO as this mystical magical creature with dark lurid secrets. Well, maybe it has some secrets, but understanding what makes SEO work and how to improve the search visibility of your Website is simple if you have the right guide.

In the pages to follow I will outline the foundational building blocks for SEO and tell you what works and what doesn't work in the field. Recently, Google introduced some major changes into how it ranks Websites; it changed its algorithms (the formulas it uses to rank Websites on its search pages). These changes are important to understand because if you don't know what you're doing, you could accidently hurt your Website's ranking rather than improve it.

This guide will bridge the divide between the complex world of SEO known only by the SEO gurus, and the everyday average Website owner simply trying to make their Website rank on Google. The following pages will give you an overview of what SEO is, in layman's terms, along with some simple strategies and techniques that you can engage in to improve your Website's ranking.

SEO takes time to see improvements. Anyone that promises you the world in a week is lying to you. Why is that? It's because Google's search engine spiders that crawl around the Web indexing all the information in existence take time to completely gather all their information. The Web is huge and Google has some safeguards in place so if you feel like you're not making progress at times, it's okay, you're not alone.

SEO didn't always involve so many different elements. It used to be much more simple and all you had to do were make some minor adjustments to your Web page, create a few links and you were done. If you did it right you could easily get page one on Google search results. Not anymore.

The Internet has grown very large, and because of that competition has increased. Naturally when you have more Websites competing for the same keywords this is going to happen. However, Google still wants to show people relevant search results and it doesn't want to have people cheat their way to the top.

If you've never had any experience with SEO, that's okay because in this guide I will deconstruct many of the components it takes to rank a Website using SEO, in layman's terms. You know, we all know the importance of being able to get free search engine traffic from Google. For the people that can master the skill, riches await on the other end of the rainbow. But, we all have to start somewhere and this guide is an excellent primer for anyone just being introduced to the SEO field.

WHO THIS BOOK IS FOR

This book is written for anyone who's just starting out in SEO or anyone with very limited knowledge of SEO that is looking to expand their understanding of it. The pages of this book will help to guide you along a beginning education of SEO and will reveal the following:

- **SEO Foundational Concepts** – The building blocks of what makes SEO work. We'll take a look at what the concepts are and how they affect your Website.

- **SEO Basic Tools & Resources** – The tools that you will use in order to implement SEO for your Website. We'll discuss what works and how to use it.

- **SEO Basic Strategies**– These are basic strategies

that you can implement, no matter what level or degree of knowledge you have in order to begin improving SEO for your site.

The SEO industry is very different today then it was even just one short year ago. The increase in competing Websites, along with the desire for Google to make the Web a better, more content-rich place has improved the Internet but has also created new limitations in SEO.

If you try to practice principals taught in older guides you might see yourself lose ranking by accidentally violating some of Google's new algorithm rules.

Google wants to see the most relevant listings show up at the top of its search engine results pages (also known as SERPs) but it also understands that people are working to optimize their listings. What Google is trying to avoid are people that know how to manipulate its set of rules to gain the upper hand on listings that use it to exploit certain products and services. For this reason, Google has introduced new limitations.

In the pages of this book I will guide you through the foundational concepts that make up SEO, what tools & resources you should use to improve your page's SEO, and how to do so.

Even if you're brand new to SEO and have never before heard of it up until today, this guide will introduce you to the concepts in a very simplified format.

1

SEO CRASH COURSE

SEO has grown into a large and diverse field. For newcomers, it can seem intimidating at first when you look at all the things that you have to do in order to reach the top of Google's search engine results pages. However, with a little bit of knowledge and the right know-how, you will be able to begin conducting SEO to make improvements to your Website.

So how does it work? Well the core foundational concept behind SEO is relevancy. Everything to Google revolves around relevancy. The search engine wants to see sites that are most relevant to the search term come up and rank highest. The less relevant Google thinks you are, the lower it will rank you. That's their desire anyway.

Over the years, it had become easy to manipulate Google's search results. People who mastered this skill were able to quickly and effectively buy a domain name, or multiple domain names, do some SEO magic, and then get it to rank page one. Of course, ranking page one is significant. Did you know that 96% of people don't go past that first page? Think about it, do you often click through to the second page of Google's search results? Most of the time you probably don't.

There are still people that know and understand Google's current algorithm and can manipulate its search results, but this takes an extraordinary amount of effort now and its not something that's as simple as it used to be.

Today, since there are so many people competing for relevancy, you really have to work hard in order to get Google to see that you're relevant. This used to be simple years ago but that's no longer the case. The amount of effort that you put into this relevancy work is going to be reflected by your position on Google's searches.

WHAT DOES RELEVANCY MEAN TO GOOGLE?

To be relevant in the eyes of Google your page must address two main factors as it relates to the search. How well you're able to address these two factors will determine your page ranking for that search. The two main factors are as follows:

- **On-Page SEO** – On-Page SEO refers to anything that can be done on the actual Website or Webpage itself to increase the relevancy of it. This includes things like optimizing the title of the page, the description, and a variety of other elements that relate to the primary keyword of the page.

- **Off-Page SEO** – This relates to how good of a job you've done to create links back to your Webpage and Website. Off-Page SEO refers to anything that's done to optimize your Website away from the Website itself. This is the largest part of SEO and takes up the most time and effort.

In order to increase your search engine visibility you must be able to optimize your page for both On-Page SEO and Off-Page SEO. I'll be covering these in some more detail in the coming chapters.

However, before diving into more concepts and instructions, it's important to note on how things have changed in the SEO world. The algorithm changes (or changes to Google's search formula) that have occurred over the course of the past couple of years have dramatically changed how a site is optimized.

Here is what's happened.

ALGORITHM CHANGE #1: GOOGLE PANDA

February 2011

Depending on how much you've already read up on SEO you may or may not have heard of the Google Panda. These so-called "Panda Attacks" are the result of a change that Google made to its algorithm dating back to February of 2011. In that algorithm change, Google's main aim was to karate chop out many of the search results that had very low quality content that violated Google's Webmaster Guidelines (found here: http://bit.ly/XeqPjN).

You see, as the years went on, search engine gurus learned how to manipulate pages to make them appear at the top of Google's search results. Naturally, this was always part of the SEO "game", however, things escalated to the point where many SEO specialists could come in and almost entirely take over the first page of Google's search results, peddling just about any product or service they chose to.

Now, Google doesn't mind it that sites address optimizing their pages to appear at the top of search results, but it did mind sites that completely bent and violated the rules to literally shove themselves up to the top of search results.

The result of all of this was the Google Panda, a major change in the way Google ranked Websites. Once it instituted these new rules, there was an immediate and dramatic shift in search results and who appeared at the top of any given search. Literally, this completely changed the search results landscape.

Depending on whom you speak to about this, they may tell you that this was a great thing, or an awful thing. Many search results experienced a dramatic change dropping some listings almost entirely off results pages that used to dominate the first page. Can you imagine the type of uproar this created?

Search engine marketers were left scrambling, trying to figure out what was going on. This resulted in huge losses of business for Websites that had low quality content with poor Website user experiences. However, this also resulted in huge gains for content rich sites that offered excellent browsing experiences and quality content.

As you can see, the focus became content and the quality of the content that's provided. This is now a cornerstone to being considered relevant by Google.

Google actually sent out many of these "Panda Attacks" (about two dozen) and they did their intended job of cleaning up the search results for relevancy. However, Google didn't just stop there.

ALGORITHM CHANGE #2: GOOGLE PENGUIN

April 2012

The Google Penguin was a much more severe algorithm change that targeted some different elements of Websites. Google knew that there was many Websites engaging in various types of elicit style SEO activities. These activities ran the gamut for finding clever ways to trick the Google search engine, but eventually they caught on.

The Google Penguin sought to punish Websites that were engaged in things like keyword stuffing (over usage of keywords), content cloaking (making a page appear different to a search engine then to a real person), and participating in link schemes, amongst many other things. These practices, and other similar ones, are today considered to be what's called Black Hat SEO techniques.

Black Hat SEO techniques are frowned upon

techniques that make you run the risk of getting demoted on Google's rankings. Black Hat SEO utilizes clever ways in fooling the search engine to think the site is more relevant then it actually is.

One example of this is some pornography sites figured out how to display different search results to the search engines then they did to real humans. Could you imagine clicking on a site you thought was about one thing, then arriving at a site, not only entirely different, but also cleverly disguised as a porn site?

In stark contrast, White Hat SEO techniques are the set of techniques involving the practice of SEO that are generally acceptable practices in the field. White Hat SEO techniques are ones that don't violate Google's Webmaster Guidelines. This book will teach you some basic White Hat SEO techniques for succeeding with Google rankings.

ALGORITHM CHANGE #3: EXACT MATCH DOMAINS

September 2012

Back in the day you could go out and purchase what you would call an exact match domain name and hit the number one spot on Google for that keyword. Not anymore.

Exact match domains (EMDs) are domain names that have the exact keyword phrase in it as the search that you're targeting. For example, iphone6rumors.com would be an exact match domain name for the keyword search "iPhone 6 Rumors". Make sense?

Today, EMDs don't work anymore unless they have other SEO value attributed to them. You see, before you could register a brand new domain that was an EMD and get it to #1 on Google without doing much else.

If you want to get ranked with these today, the EMD has to have SEO juice, meaning it has to be optimized for both On-Page and Off- Page SEO in order to rank high, just like any other Website. You can't just have an EMD domain and expect to rank #1 for that keyword anymore.

RELEVANCY

The important thing to note about these algorithm changes is what they mean for the industry moving forward. The reason why I'm highlighting these for you so early on is to drive home the importance of relevancy.

I want to tell you a quick story. When I was just a kid I enrolled in beginner's karate lessons. I took these lessons on and off for about 2 years then I stopped. Years later, during college, I re-enrolled in another karate class but this time it was in an intermediate course since I obviously knew what I was doing (or so I thought).

When I enrolled I really thought that I remembered my technique well. When we were engaged in the first day of instructions, the sensei (instructor) came over to me to watch my technique as we ran through some of the basics. I was sure I knew what I was doing. That's where I was sorely wrong.

Apparently I had the wrong technique entirely and when I kept trying to do the technique that I thought I knew so well in my head, my sensei would yell at me. This happened over and over again. It wasn't that I didn't understand what he was saying, it's that in my mind I had recalled the techniques differently so I performed them differently, or what I learned to be the wrong way.

My point in this story is that I want you to learn early on in your SEO career, the right way to do things so that later down the road you're not trying to implement the wrong techniques that will harm your site more then it will help your site. Make sense? Well, hopefully it does.

EARNING GOOGLE'S TRUST

There was a time, not so long ago, when you didn't have to earn Google's trust. You merely had it from the beginning. That was before these massive algorithm changes, also known as industry "game changers".

These game changers morphed everything. Websites went from instant trust and credibility to having to earn Google's trust. How do you have to earn Google's trust? Let me explain.

Imagine you start a new business working from home selling widgets in a town full of widget sellers. You head to the bank for a loan and pitch this incredible business plan and tell the bank manager how great your widget selling technique is going to be.

Now this is in a town that has a lot of widget sellers. There are widget sellers quite literally almost on every corner. What do you think the bank manager is going to say? Do you think he or she is going to give you a loan for a *new* widget selling business in a town already full of widget sellers? Of course not!

However, let's just say that you're a widget seller in a town full of widget sellers, but you have 5 years experience selling widgets. You have a proven track record of trust and credibility. What do you think that same bank manager is going to say when you approach this time about a bank loan? Your chances are certainly going to be much higher if not almost guaranteed!

The same principle applies to your Website listing on Google. When you register a new domain, you're telling Google that you've just opened up shop. You're the new kid on the block. Just like the bank manager, Google is not going to trust you because you're *new*. Catch what I'm throwing?

Today, Google's trust is earned, and it's a steady long road to building that trust. Google is no longer dishing out that trust so easily because it's been burned in the past for doing so.

Now today, in order to earn that trust you have to have other people that Google already trusts, link to you. What does this mean? You need links from other important Websites on the Internet that are already very trusted by Google.

However, even still, it will take time for this trust to fully develop. You can't push this trust situation overnight or very quickly. If you try to, you'll see yourself have more damage done to your listing on Google then good.

You might just end up in Google's Sandbox…

GOOGLE'S SANDBOX

As a child you probably remember playing in the sandbox. There was probably a sandbox at the park near your house or one at your school where you grew up. The sandbox was most likely a fun place for you to be where you would play with other kids or simply play on your own in the sand. Can you remember that?

Well, today, there's another little known sandbox out there. It's a sandbox that sits in Cyberspace and is a virtual place where Websites are placed when they misbehave or when they are new. This sandbox, also known as the *Sandbox Effect*, is not something you want happening to you.

If your Website is new, there's little that can be done in avoiding the Google Sandbox. While there are some ways to help your site exit Google's sandbox faster, generally speaking, if you have a pretty new domain name, then you don't have Google's trust. If you don't have Google's trust, then you have to sit in the sandbox for a while.

How long? Well, that all depends. Google won't tell anyone their exact secrets to their formulas and algorithms, but it's been estimated that this takes about 2 years to earn Google's trust. Now, this isn't 2 years from the date that you first bought your domain name. This is 2 years from the date that Google first found your domain name and listed you in its search engine. Make sense?

If you're thinking that this may not be very fair, you're probably right. What happened is some bullies came around and pushed people around the playground and now everyone has to pay for it. It's unfortunate but it's the current situation and there's not much anyone can do about it.

If you have a brand new domain, you're going to be stuck in the sandbox. It's hard to do SEO when you're stuck in the sandbox because Google filters everything that you do so that it has less impact than it normally would. This gets pretty frustrating for most people.

What advanced SEO professionals do is they buy domains that were previously owned by other people. Whether the domains were just expired domains or they buy them at auction this is a general practice that has increased in popularity recently.

Of course, for most people this really isn't an option. Usually, if you own a business and you have a domain name that you've been using for a little while you probably don't want to part with it, and rightfully so.

THE ORGANIC APPROACH

All of these facts should drive home for you the principle that Google now is very wary of newcomers to the Web. If you want Google to trust you, you have to earn it. How do you earn Google's trust? Well, that takes not only time but also having other already trusted Websites (also known as authority sites) link to you.

I wanted to tell you another story. I have this friend who's name is Jon, and Jon runs a pretty popular blog. One day I was sitting with Jon and another one of our mutual friends whose name is Mike. Mike also runs a blog. However, Mike's blog is fairly new, about 6 months old, whereas Jon's blog is just shy of 6 years old.

Well, Jon, Mike and I were all sitting in the hotel lobby waiting to attend a conference on Website usability techniques and we started talking about our Websites.

Mike, who has been working his tail off on his blog, has posted one blog nearly each and every day on his site and has done everything in his power to push it up to the top of Google. For each and every article he's written he has implemented near perfect SEO that normally should be able to get him at least to the bottom of the first page of Google. Well it hasn't.

Mike's blog has languished on Google. The best he's been able to do has been to get his blog posts onto the 3rd page of Google's search results, and even that has been a stretch for him. So, it's only obvious that this has all ended in a lot of frustration for him.

Jon on the other hand, who helped Mike get started with his blog, has had incredible success with his. Jon's blog is one of the top blogs in his niche, allowing him to generate a full time income from ads and affiliate links on it.

The most frustrating thing for Mike has been that Jon actually taught Mike everything that he does with his blog. He showed him all the ways he researches his keywords, how he optimizes his pages, where he creates his links, literally everything. These are all the same techniques that Jon uses to consistently rank his blog's articles at the top of the first page of Google, almost every single time.

What Jon didn't realize is that he has a trusted domain (also known as an aged domain). Jon's blog has been around for a while so it not only has its age going for it but it has received thousands of important back links from other trusted Websites on the Internet. This is the reason why Jon's blog posts always soar to the top rankings on Google whenever he posts them but Mike's doesn't.

AGED DOMAINS

As we were sitting there talking about this I smiled to myself. I thought, wow, most people don't know about aged domains. After explaining the rules to Mike and Jon they both looked at me as if they had come to an incredible epiphany.

One was in shock and the other one was in joy. Can you guess which one acted in which way? Yes, Jon was happy that his advice wasn't entirely wrong, but Mike was angry that he hadn't known this from the start.

It wasn't always like this. Those Google algorithm changes literally changed everything and this new recognition of the domain's age was part of those major changes. Can you see how not understanding something entirely in the beginning or trying to use the wrong technique can hinder you or even hurt you?

Mike could have saved himself a lot of headache if he had simply purchased an aged domain name at auction. Yes, that's possible and it's a technique that a lot of professional SEOs do today, but this too needs to be approached with tact and delicacy as part of a wider overall SEO strategy. Because when you buy a domain name at auction, you're buying Google's trust, but this should only be attempted by professional SEOs.

Did the light bulb go off in your head? If you have a brand new domain name and you've done some SEO work but haven't been able to rank, this could be one of the causes. But, one thing to note here is that you can't just buy any domain name that's "aged" it has to be one that Google had already indexed in the past (one that has already been in its search results).

Of course, this is slightly beyond the scope of our discussion here but it's important information that you at least are aware of. The important thing to understand and take away from this is that in the beginning if you try to do SEO the wrong way, you can cost yourself a lot of headache, a lot of time, a lot of money, and or all of the above.

AUTHORITY

During that same conversation, Mike, Jon, and I began talking more about what makes a Website actually rank at the top of Google searches. What Mike failed to teach Jon was that he created something called an authority domain. What's an authority domain? It's when your domain name reaches a certain level of importance by receiving a lot of links from other important domains.

During the course of Jon's 6 years of blogging he did a lot of linking to his blog. He went out there and wrote articles on other Websites that were popular, he made videos on YouTube that he embedded on his site, he posted links to his various blog articles in forums on the Internet, he wrote as a guest blogger on other blogs, and so much more. In return for doing all of this work, he was able to get a lot of other important Websites to start linking back to his content.

We sat there listening to Jon speak and Mike seemed fairly impressed. There was a lot of work involved over those 6 years. Over those 6 years that Jon was blogging he created his domain into an authority domain. Not only has he been around for a while writing unique blogs every week that are well-researched but he did an exhaustive amount of work getting other important Websites to link to him. He created authority.

2

KEYWORD RESEARCH

When did it first happen for you? When did you first find out about SEO? If you're like some people, you always knew it existed but probably felt very intimidated by it. For many business owners and non-business owners alike, SEO is a complicated thing. It involves a bunch of complex programming languages, calculations, and techniques right? Well, not really.

SEO can be made simple, very simple, if you know what you're doing. Aside from understanding the importance of building trust with Google, you have to know how to create a page that, once you've built that trust, can rank at the top of search results.

So how's it done?

To get started you have to know what you're aiming at. Whatever product or service you have to offer there's a keyword that fits it. This keyword is either one word or a group of words combined into a phrase. The keyword is what you enter into Google's search when you're trying to find the answer to something or you're searching out some other type of information.

SEO is simple once you know the keyword you're targeting. You can't just shoot in the dark. Having the right information will make the difference between success and failure.

Let's go back to the example of the widget seller for a moment, but this time we'll put a different spin on it. Let's just say that we have a different widget seller one who lives out in the country because he became so frustrated with living in a big crowded city. This country widget seller sells a special type of widgets that you can't find everywhere. His widgets, he's come to realize, are also in very high demand in this country town.

Our new country widget seller has so much business that on some days he has to turn people away. There are a lot of people looking for the widgets that he has but not a lot of people offering them, ending up with little to no competition for him. That's supply and demand for you right there. Well, the same thing holds true for keywords.

When there's a keyword that has a lot of competition (aka there are a lot of widget sellers out there) it's going to be much harder for you to compete, especially if Google doesn't already trust you. If there is little competition for the search, just like our country widget seller, you'll be living life on easy street.

If you do the research and find out what keywords have low competition but high demand you will have a much easier time doing SEO for your Website. On the other hand however, if you try to enter a highly competitive field with low demand then you won't do well. You won't know what type of keyword yours is unless you do the research.

To do keyword research doesn't require a lot of effort or knowhow. In fact, it involves leveraging existing tools already provided by Google itself. Without a tool like this it would be difficult to gauge and understand what keywords to target. You wouldn't know how much competition there was and you wouldn't know how many people are searching for them.

RESEARCHING KEYWORDS

To research keywords all you have to do is use a tool that
Google provides for you. It's called the Google Keyword
Tool and you can find it right here: http://bit.ly/VdVzS4.

When you get to the page all you need to do is type in your keyword. Let's say you were selling homemade candles. You would simply type in "homemade candles" in the box given to you and begin your search. Google will tell you the following after you hit the search button:

- How much competition the keyword has – Low, Medium or High

- How many local searches happen per month

- How many global searches happen per month

- How many other similar keywords there are to that one

Here's an example of a search done using the Google Keyword Tool. This search is done for "how to make money online," a very competitive field to enter. You can see by the results returned that your best bet would be to go with a variation of that keyword such as "make money online from home." This is what you call a long-tail keyword.

A long tail keyword is usually easier to target then its shorter counterparts. Why do you think that is? Well, as you can see from the image of search results for "how to make money online," far less people are searching for "make money online from home," then they are for the keyword that was entered into the search.

However, it's better to come up closer to the top of Google search results then it is to be left withering away on page 2, 3 or beyond. Using long-tail keywords to optimize a Webpage should be something to consider if you're still trying to build Google's trust.

When you're researching a keyword, especially when you still don't have Google's trust, you really should try to target keywords with LOW competition and higher monthly search volumes. You might have difficulty finding these but time spent in this stage is time well spent and will pay off handsomely if you can reach the top of a search.

PICKING YOUR PRIMARY KEYWORD

Picking your primary keyword is important. It's basically your message to Google telling it what your Webpage is all about. Keep in mind that this primary keyword is what you're going to optimize your page around. Most of the little bits and pieces of your SEO work will be geared towards making Google understand that this is what your page is about.

For the most part, you will not be able to compete on keywords that have MEDIUM or HIGH competition, especially early on. Unless you have a domain that is aged and has some authority, don't focus on those. Pick one keyword with LOW competition, even if it has to be a long-tail keyword; this will be your primary keyword that you will want to target.

When you pick your primary keyword it's important to

understand that you will write content that falls in line with this keyword. For this reason, try not to pick a primary keyword that will be hard to use in sentences (yes a lot of those exist out there).

OPTIMIZING FOR YOUR KEYWORD

About a year back, I was having a conversation with this woman that I met at a local coffee shop. She was sitting at the table next to me talking on the telephone with what sounded like her Web developer. I was trying not to pry but I remember her asking him some questions and being seemingly frustrated by the answers.

When the woman (whose name was Mary) hung up the phone I struck up a conversation with her. I asked her what the problem with her Website was. Mary then went on to begin telling me about all the problems that she's had ranking her Website on Google.

I guess I had heard this before but I listened to her until she was done speaking and then began asking her some questions.

During the conversation Mary explained to me all of

the frustrations she has had and during the brief chat I was able to gather the following information from her:

- Mary had an existing business and Website.

- Her Website was originally built 4 years prior to our conversation.

- She was having difficulty ranking on the first page of Google.

- She had her Website redesigned by her Web developer.

- Her Web developer also promised to help her rank on Google.

So, what I was able to learn from Mary was that she was in pretty good shape. She had a Website that had been on Google for about 4 years but wasn't ranking very high so she decided to hire a Web developer to fix that. By being around for 4 years she had built some trust with Google. However, although her Web developer redesigned a beautiful Website for her, he tried for months to get her to rank but he was unable to do so. What was the problem?

It was clear from our conversation that the Web designer was not an SEO specialist. The problem is that finding a person who can both do very good design and also understand SEO is difficult. That's why it's important to be educated.

I sat there listening to Mary talk about her business and

saw how excited she was by it all, but every time she referred to her Website she seemed to get upset. What I found heart wrenching was, here was a woman who was so passionate about business but felt stuck because she just didn't know what she was doing. Sound familiar? I can tell you first hand that I've met many people in this same exact situation.

BUILDING AUTHORITY

Mary and I spoke for a while and I explained the basics to her. I told her that although she had Google's trust, it sounded like she needed help with On-Page SEO as well as some Off-Page SEO. She seemed confused, which is understandable. Most Website owners don't understand what it takes to rank on Google. I informed her that it wasn't just one of the many factors that would boost her up Google's rankings, she needed to address them all.

Mary's Website developer had done a fine job of redesigning her Website. It looked "cool" as she put it. In fact it was a beautifully designed Website, one of the best I had seen in a while. However, as most unseasoned Web designers, he didn't know much about SEO. How did this hurt Mary? Well, for starters, the Web designer made a lot of the text as images. Google can't read text in images. He created a beautiful looking Website but also sacrificed her ability to rank high in the process.

He knew how to create cool looking Websites, but he didn't know how to build that Website so it best addressed SEO. It's my guess that many people have run into this same scenario in the past.

After we were done having our conversation she hired me to completely take over her Website and search engine optimization work. Well, needless to say, I was able to get her to #1 on Google for her service, but it took nearly 3 months for this to happen even though there was low competition for her keyword.

I'll explain in a bit more detail, but for now, I'll be covering some more of the basics of what SEO involves and I'll be showing you just what you have to do for your own Website to begin building that authority I spoke of earlier. Without authority you will rank nowhere fast.

SEO THE RIGHT WAY

If you're worried that SEO is going to be a lot of work, well, yes, you're right. SEO is a lot of work. However, there are some shortcuts but depending on what shortcuts you take you risk the possibility of not ranking as high by not taking a fully "organic" approach.

What does that mean? It means that if you don't invest yourself into doing the work over a period of time, then Google will figure out that you're trying to force and "scheme" your way up the top and it will most likely penalize you for that.

For example, let's just say that there's a new Website. Today that Website has a total of zero links to it. Well, let's just say that I decide to go out there and have someone create a whole lot of links for me then I go tell Google about these links by pinging them all at the same time.

Well, if there's a Website that had zero links a month ago, then one month later it has thousands of new links, and especially if these links are from non-authority domains, Google will know you're cheating. Once Google figures this out you will be sandboxed. This was one of the main goals and aims of the Google Penguin.

My desire for you with this book is to not only help you learn and understand just what SEO is all about and the pieces that make it work, but I want you to understand how to do *SEO the right way*. It's so easy to get lost and confused in this industry. There's so many so-called gurus yelling and shouting from the mountaintop, telling you what to do and how to do it but those gurus sometimes have their own personal agendas.

Sure, at the end of the day everyone wants to make money, but it's still surprising to me how much misinformation and disinformation still exists in the field of SEO. Most people want you to know only just enough to have a conversation about it, but not actually enough to help yourself. Of course these are most of the same people trying to sell you their own products and services.

For this reason, it's important to educate yourself first. Once you have an overview of knowledge in SEO you can confidently go out there and hire someone to help you and actually know what it is that they're doing and whether or not you're being "taken to town" on the project.

The SEO industry is also fast paced and rapidly changing. As you can tell by the recent algorithm changes that I relayed to you, things change so fast that it's important you try to stay up to date with what's going on. Not only that, but it's also important to understand just how it all works before you try to dive in head first and possibly make some costly mistakes you may end up regretting.

3

ON-PAGE SEO

During my conversation with Mary at the coffee shop we talked in great detail about what it took to rank a site. The reason she hired me on the spot was that I took the time to explain to her how SEO worked, something she said no one else had taken the time to do. This brief, yet informative conversation would have never have happened if I hadn't have overheard her conversation.

Once I got a clear understanding for where her site stood, I told her what it would take to get her to rank. She didn't understand the first thing it took to optimize her pages with Google. But, then again, most people don't.

After talking for a while and looking at her site on my laptop in the coffee shop, the complete picture begun to take shape for me. Mary's site was in need of a lot of help.

Even though her Website had been redesigned to look beautiful, it wasn't configured properly for keywords, page names and it was too heavy on the graphics for starters. Yes, her Website had some authority because she was a trusted domain that had been around for a few years, however, not much else was going in her favor.

This was to Mary's dismay. She thought she was getting a final product that would not only look nice but would also help her rank as well. Unfortunately, she didn't, and I've seen this happen time and time again. When a person doesn't know the first thing about SEO how are they supposed to know what they're looking for in a case like a Website redesign? They don't.

All of the elements that I found wrong with Mary's Website have to do with On-Page SEO. These are things that occur on the actual Website itself, as opposed to Off-Page SEO, which refers to SEO done away from the Website. Mary's On-Page SEO was in need of serious help but it wasn't going to be as much of an effort as would be involved in Off- Page SEO.

ON-PAGE OPTIMIZATION REQUIREMENTS

During my brief chat with Mary I gave her a breakdown of how On-Page SEO worked. I explained that On-Page SEO was much easier to tackle than Off- Page SEO and after looking at her "cool" Website I easily spotted several key elements that weren't being addressed properly.

It's difficult for someone like Mary to have known any of this without my help. I guess it's a little bit like hiring a mechanic or a repairman. When you don't understand what you're dealing with, you can't really be sure if someone is being straightforward with you or not.

I took a look at one of her Webpages that was describing a service that her company was offering. Mary's company, by the way, provides professional resume writing services for career seeking individuals. The Webpage didn't address and meet all of the requirements for On-Page SEO Optimization.

Here are all the On-Page SEO requirements that need to be addressed:

1. **Page URL**: The Webpage's URL must have the primary keyword in it separated by hyphens. This can be done in Wordpress by turning on something called permalinks and using the "postname" option in Wordpress so that it creates all the pages with the page or article title.

2. **Title of Page**: The Webpage's title tag must have the primary keyword in it and be no longer then 70 characters. If you have permalinks turned on in Wordpress on as per #1, then the placing the primary keyword in the title will also translate to the page URL. This is the title that shows up in the listing when you search Google.

3. **Page Description**: The Webpage's description (also known as the meta description) must have the primary keyword in it and be no longer then 140 characters. This description is the description that shows up in the listing when you search Google.

4. **Page Content**: The Webpage must have at least 500 words of well-researched unique content, and preferably 1000 words to rank high.

5. **Keyword Density**: The Webpage must have a keyword density of at least 2% and no more then 5% - this refers to the number of times your keyword appears on the page versus how many words of content there are. If you have 1000

words on your page your keyword should appear at least 20 times for a 2% keyword density.

6. **Heading Tags**: The Webpage must have the primary keyword in three separate heading tags, H1, H2, and H3. If you use Wordpress you can highlight your text and select the Heading1, Heading2, or Heading3 options from the drop down of expanded options in the editor.

7. **Keyword Styling**: The Webpage must have the primary keyword stylize in bold font, italics font and underlined font.

8. **Image ALT Tags**: Google can't read text in images, so it's important that when you add an image to your Webpage it has an ALT tag attribute. This is the alternative text tag and it needs to have your primary keyword in it. Anytime you add an image through Wordpress you will be able to enter in an ALT tag for it.

9. **External Links**: If the Webpage has any links going out to other Websites they should have a "Nofollow" attribute – this basically tells Google's spiders not to follow the link, making your Webpage more important because it all the links stop there. This is different then "Dofollow".

10. **Internal Links**: The Webpage should have a link within the content to another page on the same domain name.

Mary came to the realization that her Webpage didn't address half of the requirements for On-Page SEO after I got done explaining them to her. She was frustrated but overall glad that she at least knew what to look for now.

If you have a Webpage, or you've created a Webpage in the past, compare and contrast the points above with your content. Do you meet most of the requirements for an optimized page? If not, what are you missing?

It's easy to address most of the items on the list if you have the right tools to do so. If you're using Wordpress there are several plugins that are available that can help you along. However, needless to say, the more detail oriented and careful you are here with addressing all of the elements for On-Page SEO, the better your overall results will be.

Keep this list as a handy guide nearby and refer to it when you go back to writing the content for your Website. It will take time to be able to successfully tackle some of the items in the list. For example, item #5 is keyword density and achieving a keyword density of 2% is hard, especially when you don't want it to come across sounding "spammy".

OVER-OPTIMIZATION WARNING

With the release of the Google Panda & the Google Penguin, Google has become very particular with sites that are attempting to over-optimize their content. If your content does not sound natural and it looks like your keywords are too forced, you will not rise in the rankings, and risk being demoted for those particular search keywords.

When you are writing your content, keep it very natural sounding. You do not have to use your keyword in the exact search term in each section. You can do variations from time to time, which will in fact help you rank higher. This is called LSI, or Latent Semantic Indexing. LSI is a technology used by Google to determine similar words and phrasing for search terms, but don't beat yourself up trying to force your keyword term in each area. Keep it as natural sounding as possible for the best results.

WORDPRESS PLUG-INS FOR ON-PAGE SEO

If you're using Wordpress to manage & update your Website then there are a lot of very useful plugins that you can download and use to help you with On-Page SEO. The problem with Wordpress on its own is that it doesn't allow you the flexibility to edit some of the fields that you need to be able to edit in order to achieve full 100% optimization. One example is the meta description, or page description field discussed in item #3 for On-Page SEO requirements. Wordpress doesn't give you the flexibility to change this by default for each page or article post that you create.

Installing a plugin is a great way to simplify your life. There are several that are excellent for SEO. The one that I always end up defaulting to is SEOPressor. This is a paid plugin that you can find by clicking this very obvious affiliate link right here: http://bit.ly/seopressorv5 or you can simply Google "seopressor" and find it that way.

If you don't want to spend the money on it there are some free plugins that are also available. Here's a free plugin from Yoast: http://bit.ly/13r5Q0C that won't do everything the paid plugin above will but it will allow you to at least change the page description field for each post or page you create in Wordpress.

4

OFF-PAGE SEO

About a year ago I took a trip to the Bay Islands just off the coast of Honduras, home to the largest barrier reef in the Caribbean. The Bay Islands are very well known for excellent diving because of this barrier reef and most people go out for weeklong excursions of diving in some of the most pristine waters in the world.

I was pretty excited to say the least and although I'm a very amateur diver what was most important about that trip was a realization that I came to on the flight in. As the small plane that left from the mainland of Honduras was circling the island and coming in for a landing I drew a very interesting comparison.

In this world there are a lot of islands. Some of these islands we know about and some of these islands we don't know about. What I found most interesting about my observation was how much this is similar to Websites on the Internet.

When you first start out a new Website, you're like a lonely little island, sitting somewhere out in the sea. In the beginning no one knows about this island. In Cyberspace, there are millions and millions of these tiny islands (new Websites), along with some larger islands (popular Websites) and a few continents (very well known Websites like Google & Facebook).

If you could imagine just for a moment what this would look like in your mind. Then picture small bridges connecting all of these islands. Those small bridges are links on the Internet.

In this imaginary picture in your mind, also picture some bigger bridges similar to the ones you would find connecting some of the largest islands in the world such as Manhattan. These bigger bridges come from the bigger Websites with high page rank. Can you see how these bigger bridges would bring in a lot more traffic to the islands?

This is what Off-Page SEO is. You're building these virtual bridges, or links, to your Website, an island sitting out there somewhere in Cyberspace. If your island has been around for a while then it's already been mapped and trusted by Google. But when it's new, Google is still wary of it. These islands pop up all over the place in Cyberspace every minute of every day.

Building these virtual bridges takes time. It's a concentrated effort on your part to go out there and build links. But it's not just about the quantity of bridges that you build; it's also about the quality. For example, a bridge from a Website like YouTube is far more valuable then a bridge from a low trafficked blog or forum Website. Does this make sense? Hopefully it does.

This part of SEO takes the most time and effort. Optimizing your Webpage is one thing, but having to go out there and constantly build these virtual bridges by commenting on forums, shooting and posting videos on YouTube, sharing links on social media, and all the other activities that makeup Off-Page SEO takes time, a lot of time.

For some people, they don't mind because they have lots of time on their hands in the first place. But for most other people (myself included), time is a precious commodity and there is little to waste. But since link relationships are one of the building blocks to Internet SEO this is a very important aspect that has a big impact on your Website's visibility.

BUILDING LINKS TO YOUR WEBSITE

A few months ago I went to this meet-up group that I found online. It was a group of business owners that were interested in meeting to discuss different marketing ideas. I was curious to see what everyone else out there in the world was doing to tackle online marketing so I said what the heck and I went.

When I headed for the little café that day to meet the group I had just been through a long and exhausting phone call with a client about her Website. It was another new referral, and yet another new person who was completely lost when it came to optimizing her Website. Strolling to the café I thought of the conversation and thought about just how little average people know about SEO.

Coming from her and the other people that I speak to,

SEO is a scary thing that they don't even dare to tackle. Besides, most people are too busy working <u>in</u> their businesses as opposed to working <u>on</u> their businesses. However, building links to your Website, also considered to be one of the hardest parts of SEO work, can be simplified if you tackle it for an hour or two a day.

The part that overwhelms most people is the thought of all the work they need to put in to get ranked on Google. But with a little bit of effort each and every single day, over time you will make progress. What's more is that Google will see that this is being done naturally and that you're not going out there and using some program to create thousands and thousands of links back to your site. It knows the difference when a link looks organic or if some automated system placed it there. While many professional SEOs do this, unless you know exactly what you're doing you could risk hurting your site more then helping it. So be wary!

SEO isn't really all that complicated. It's more that SEO just takes good clean effort. But, if you're willing to roll up your sleeves and get busy building content and creating links, you will see huge differences in your rankings.

WHY LINKS ARE IMPORTANT

It's hard to get Google to trust a Website. Although you may be new to SEO it's important to understand the importance of building high quality links to your site. By doing this, you're telling Google that you matter because other people that matter are linking to you. That's just the way it works.

It's almost like a high school popularity contest. The cool kids will rank up at the top because everyone knows them or has heard of them. While this may sound childish, it's true. When other important sites link back to your site, you bridge the gap of trust building.

Building trust doesn't happen overnight. Google is not going to trust a brand new domain name no matter how many high quality sites are linking to it, especially if this happens very quickly. Why is that? Google knows that these are some of the tricks that people try to institute and it does what it can to stop this from happening.

Your best way of building trust for your Website is by creating links back to your own Website from other important sites gradually, over a period of time. This will happen naturally as you build content, create YouTube videos, comment on forums, and so on.

BUILDING YOUR FIRST LINKS

When I got to the meet-up that afternoon I was pleased to see a really good turnout. There were about 30 different business people from all types of businesses that had one important thing in common: they all had a Website.

We all sat at a large table and opened up a discussion about marketing. Since this is something that is one of the most challenging subjects for small businesses owners, everyone was keen to find out what the other person was doing in terms of online marketing. We went around the table and we all checked off what we were doing. A lot of the most common responses to online marketing seemed to be through the following four major sites:

- Facebook

- Twitter

- Google Plus

- LinkedIn

There's probably a big reason for this. Why do you think that is? Well it seems like social media has taken over our lives. This isn't a bad thing, but I wanted to explain to you why this is important.

Social media sites like Facebook, Twitter and Google Plus are what you call authority domains. LinkedIn fits up there as well due to its recent introduction of a newsfeed and the ability to share links and other details with your connections. In fact, these are very high-ranking authority domains. On the Internet, you can measure the importance of a domain name with something called page rank. Websites like Facebook, Twitter, LinkedIn and Google Plus have very high page ranks.

Page rank is measured out of a total possible number of 10. Google's home page is considered a 10 because it is the most highly trafficked Website in the world. Facebook is also a page rank of 10. Why does this matter? Remember that whole thing about building Google's trust? Well that happens by getting links from high page rank Websites (trusted Websites) like these four, back to you.

There are of course other ways to begin building page rank, but having good links from these types of sites is an excellent way to start. But that's not all Google wants to see. Google wants to see a good mixture of links to your site, not just from the big social media sites. Not only that but Google wants to see links to different pages on your site, and not just the home page.

GETTING OTHER PEOPLE TO LINK TO YOU

During the meet-up, before we were all going around the table introducing ourselves and sharing our ideas, I started talking to a guy named Paul. Paul runs a t-shirt business. He creates silkscreen t-shirts in his garage then sells them on his Website.

Paul and I started speaking about his business and began chatting about different things that he does to market his site online. Although Paul only knew some of the basics of SEO he did understand the bigger picture of online marketing.

Something intrigued me that Paul told me he does. Paul creates different design ideas so that people can choose which one they like best. He makes a contest. He hosts this contest on his Facebook business page but the contest links to three different pages on his Website. These three different pages each contain one design variation of a shirt, which he has written a blog about. He has people vote on, or like, which shirt design they like best by hitting the like button on that specific article page and sharing it through social media.

Why is this important? Paul doesn't realize it but he's doing something called creating link bait. He's put something out onto the Web with the purpose of building more links to it. He didn't really do it on purpose but he told me after the first time he did it he had such a great response and noticed that people were finding the shirt designs and pages in Google searches and decided to keep it going.

Paul was a master online marketer without even knowing it. I found this extremely interesting and very educational.

Why is this important? Well, what happens here is that when enough people are linking to your page or content, it's telling Google the level of importance that content has and in turn increasing Google's trust in that page. If hundreds or even thousands of people like or share a link, what type of message do you think that's conveying to Google? It's a pretty strong one.

There are different types of link bait that you can create. Have you ever noticed on Instagram or on Facebook how you come across these ingenious photos with popular quotes on them? These photos make you laugh, cry, or anything in between, and you just need to share it with everyone you know. Has this ever happened to you? Of course it has.

What these clever ingenious people are doing is creating link bait. When something like that goes viral or is shared a certain amount of times it builds link bridges and trust in the eyes of Google. Most of those images are either linked to a specific account on Instagram for example, or on a Website that it was originally shared from and now it's getting re-shared thousands of times over and over again. This is enormous trust and credibility building.

These are just some examples of the ways that you can go about getting people to link to you but there are hundreds of different ideas you can institute when it comes to creating link bait but the whole purpose here is to get people linking to your Website to begin building that trust and credibility with Google.

When link baiting is done right and the link points to a page that has been perfectly optimized with all of the On-Page SEO requirements I discussed earlier, the results can be tremendous.

LINKING STRATEGIES

During our meet-up group, the ideas filtered in. Beyond the three major social media sites, and of course LinkedIn, different people were engaging in a variety of different marketing efforts both online and offline. However a lot of the people at the table seemed frustrated with their online efforts. They were putting in a lot of work but not noticing a lot of return. Does this sound familiar?

Off-Page SEO is basically a lot of link building. You're trying to build as many links from as many different types of Websites as you possibly can. This can be hard in the beginning and can take a lot of time. To start, create these links from other sites that Google trusts.

You can use the following high page rank Websites:

- Facebook.com

- Twitter.com

- Plus.Google.com

- LinkedIn.com

- Folkd.com

- Stumbleupon.com

- Pintrest.com

- Zootool.com

- Springpad.com

- Oneview.com

- Diigo.com

- Delicious.com

- Reddit.com

- Blinklist.com

The first and most important way to start creating these links is by embedding a link to your Website in your online profile of each of these sites. These are very important high page ranking links back to your own Website and will begin to help build authority and trust with Google.

Once you've created profile links try to check in and share information and links back to your own personal or business Website every few days. It may sound like a lot of work, and it can be, but if you simply setup a schedule for yourself in your calendar to send yourself reminders to do the work in small chunks it will be much easier. Rotate the sites so you do four one day, four the next, four the day after, and so on. Of course, you can pick another schedule that works for you, but just make sure however you do it that you stick to it and be consistent.

Finally, don't try to do all the links on one day. It's much better if you do this over time so that you can begin building up that trust and credibility with Google gradually. This is one of those things that you can't force and pushing out a ton of links all at the same time will show Google that you're trying to cheat your way to the top. It has to happen naturally and organically to build trust and make your site more relevant.

CONTENT MARKETING

Before we finished the round robin of speakers at the little online marketing meet-up that I attended the gavel came to me to speak. I had listened to what everyone had to say and was the second to last person to share my ideas.

I informed everyone that what they were all doing sounded great and that for each specific person the strategy would be different depending on their personalities, but I didn't hear many people speak about content marketing.

Content marketing is not the same thing as what Paul and I had discussed prior to the meet-up starting. Content marketing is something entirely different and it's something that can really improve the search engine visibility of your Website.

First of all, you have to make sure that all your On-Page SEO is addressed. It needs to be spot on in order for you to have the *potential* to rank high. If you don't have that, then don't start doing Off-Page SEO until you're sure your page is in perfect order.

As I sat there and explained to them my strategies for content marketing, they all looked at me in a bit of bewilderment. They didn't understand how building content away from your Website was helpful.

Here's how it works.

Content marketing is when you go to other very high page ranking Websites and you build content. This content then links back to your Website. What kind of content? It can be anything. For example, you can post a blog, you can post a Word document, or you can even post a PowerPoint presentation of your content.

When you post content and you optimize that content with your newly formed On-Page SEO skills, and you link that well-researched unique content back to your Website, it brings huge improvement to the SEO value of your site. Why?

Well, first off, these Websites have very high page ranks, but aside from that, when you create content that has value on a popular site, lots of people will see it, and lots of people will most likely hit the like button, share it, tweet it, and so on. This content then has a link, with your primary keyword, back to the page on your Website that you're trying to optimize. See where this is heading?

If you can make a piece of content popular on a very popular site, then link that content back to you, that is huge in terms of Off-Page SEO link building. Important pieces of unique content that are well written and well researched that link back to you should be one of your primary aims in your Off-Page SEO efforts.

Content marketing can be done on dozens of sites throughout the Internet. However, these are the most popular, highest page ranking sites of the group that I personally like to use:

- Squidoo.com

- Tumblr.com

- Slideshare.com

- HubPages.com

- Scribd.com

- YouTube.com

Before you start building this content, you have to make sure that your own Webpage is optimized for the keyword that you're targeting. Remember the basic On-Page SEO requirements?

Your Webpage should be optimized before you start building content to it. However, once you do start building content towards an optimized page you use your own primary keyword from the content site. This then creates a strong bond between the two sites because both the content site has been optimized for the primary keyword along with your site as well.

While the basis for content marketing may sound

simple, don't misunderstand how powerful of a tool this is to increase the search engine visibility of your Website. You should immediately tackle content marketing and begin building content that links back to your own Website from authority sites.

PINGING

A friend of mine told me a story a few months ago. He had recently gotten into an argument with his wife and he was rather upset at the moment. My friend, whose name is Steve, works for an aerospace company as an electrical engineer. He's been with the same company for eight years now.

Steve is a pretty detail oriented person. I'm not sure if you know the type I'm talking about but he's the kind of person that paid attention to every single detail of something. He could always remember the strangest facts regarding just about anything. If you sent him an email telling him you would do something in a certain way, and then did it differently, he would quickly call you out on it. Yeah, he's that guy.

Anyhow, Steve 's argument with his wife was over an

award that he received at work. He was recognized for excellence in his field of electrical engineering and he was awarded employee of the year by his employer. Along with a small celebration at the office, Paul received a glowing letter and certificate, which he hung above his desk in his office at home so that his wife would see it.

Well, a day went by and his wife didn't say anything to him about it. He had figured she would say something but she didn't mention it entirely. This upset Steve immensely and it was the basis for their argument. He explained to me how insensitive and selfish his wife was for not caring about the award he received at work.

Later that night when he went home, he and his wife got into a long heated battle. It turns out that she never saw the letter in the office, because he never told her about it. She was busy that day with chores and running around the town and didn't have a chance to go into the office to tidy up like she does most days.

Steve was embarrassed to say the least. Of course, if he had told his wife about it she would have gone in and found the letter and the certificate and of course she would have been ecstatic for him.

My point in the story is that if Steve told his wife about the letter she would have went in and found it hanging above the desk and been able to read it. Well, the same thing applies on the Internet.

Sometimes you have to tell Google to go and read the information on a Webpage. This is because Google doesn't visit every page on the Internet everyday because that would be virtually impossible. This is also especially the case if a Website does not have a high page rank, or authority.

For Websites that have high page rank, Google visits them often. For example, Google visits Amazon's Website often, most likely hourly. But, what do you do in the case where you want to tell Google about a link and you don't want to wait around until it decides to visit the site? You do something called pinging.

To ping a link to Google basically tells the search engine's spiders to go crawl the information on that page. Did you know that Google doesn't crawl 95% of links that have no page rank or very low page rank? Yes, that's true. So sometimes you have to tell Google to stop in for a visit.

If Steve had told his wife to go in and read the letter, she would have gladly read it and celebrated with him, but he didn't.

In order to ping a link to Google you can use a multitude of pinging services out there. One that I like to use, which is free service, is called Pingler.com. Pingler also has a paid service that you can use if you feel so inclined. I personally have a paid account with Pingler.com but I would recommend it either way.

With a paid account on Pingler, you can instruct Google to keep coming back to the site every few days (whatever number you tell it to). This works best for sites like blogs and others that have their content updated frequently.

Each time that I write a blog post, or I want to have Google visit a link for something that I wrote I add the link to my Pingler account. This is something that you should do yourself as well, otherwise Google may not visit your site for a long time, and this will lengthen the time it takes to get ranked.

PROCEEDING WITH CAUTION

One important thing to note here is that when creating links from sites like authority sites, it's easy to go overboard. What does this mean? It's easy to go out there, get very excited about your site and start spamming a ton of links within moments of each other through all of the social media sites available. This is not a good thing.

It's okay to take one article or one piece of content from your site and share it across as many different platforms as possible. However, don't do this for multiple articles each day. As much as you think you will be helping your site, you may in fact be hindering it by over posting. This is something that the Google Penguin targeted and it's something that you need to be aware of.

Sometimes in the wake of these new Google SEO rules, you're going to feel like you're walking a bit of a tight

rope because you are. You don't want to overdo it or you'll
end up in the Sandbox and that's not where you want to
be, especially if you already have an aged domain. Take it
easy with the posting and allow it to happen naturally and
organically. Post a few articles or content each week and
share each of those as much as possible.

I will be discussing some techniques to use some
syndication services that are available for sharing your
content across different social media networks
automatically in coming chapters. For now, just keep in
mind that everything you do should be done as naturally
and organically as possible to not rock the boat. This holds
especially true if your site has no links to it when you start
out.

Google keeps track of all of these things along with
your link acceleration – or the pace at which the number
of links that you have increases each month. Basically,
Google keeps track of everything related to your site, all
the time. It's like Big Brother watching over you now so be
aware of that and always keep it in the back of your mind.

5

CONTENT IS KING

On the Internet today, content means everything. I remember going back to my conversation in the hotel lobby with Jon and Mike discussing all of the different ways that Mike was going about trying to SEO his site.

Jon had taught Mike the importance of almost all things SEO including how important it was to write good content. As Mike explained his blog to us that day he described in detail how much work he put in to writing good content. He would spend the right amount of time researching the answers to things before setting about to write an article that gave advice.

Google knows how well researched your content is and it knows how unique it is. If you try to duplicate content from other sources you are going to lose in the ranking game. You have to take the time and put in the effort to really set out and provide value for people. Without doing that you won't win on ranking with Google searches.

Not only does Mike spend the time writing really good content, he also puts in the care and effort in optimizing his content as well. Now if only Mike had a domain that had some age and authority he would be really winning at the ranking game. However, I think, over time that Mike's site will drastically improve, just as yours will.

By taking simple efforts each and everyday to put out good unique content that's properly optimized for On-Page SEO and is properly linked to by other authority sites, you will watch your rankings soar.

Of course, if you're one step ahead of the game and you have an older Website that has been listed on Google for a while, then your ability to rank high just went up dramatically. Consider yourself lucky.

Remember that SEO takes a lot of commitment and effort on your part. It's easy to want to give up and throw in the towel at times, but just keep at it and don't allow yourself to get discouraged. Your changes will take time to show up on Google's search engine. Like the example with Mary's Website, even though there was low competition for her keyword it still took me the better part of three months to get her to the top of her search.

CONTINUED SEO EDUCATION

I truly hope that you enjoyed this book on SEO and I hope that it has illuminated some light on an all too often shrouded trade. My hope is that is that it educated you and provided a better look at an industry that may have once seemed confusing to you.

The purpose of my creating this book was to provide some of the basic principles and strategies involved in the SEO field. There is a lot to learn, but now that you have the basics covered, I would recommend checking out either of the two other books in this three-part SEO Series. You can find either the *SEO White Book*, or the *SEO Black Book* useful in providing a more advanced look at SEO and the specific tactics to ranking high on Google.

OTHER BOOKS BY THIS AUTHOR

I would really appreciate it if you could take a few moments and share your thoughts by posting a review on Amazon. I put a lot of care into the books that I write and I hope that this care and sincerity come across in my writing.

Here is the link to post a review for *SEO Simplified – Learn Search Engine Optimization Strategies and Principles for Beginners*: http://www.amazon.com/dp/B00BN7PGEY

If you're thinking about writing and publishing your own work on Amazon's Kindle, please take a look at my other book entitled *Kindle Marketing Ninja Guide – Killer Marketing Strategies for Kindle Book Marketing Success* or *Kindle Self Publishing Gold – Unlocking the Secrets of How to Make Money Online with Kindle eBooks*.

- *SEO White Book – The Organic Guide to Google Search Engine Optimization* - *http://www.amazon.com/dp/B00BUOPFHI*

- *SEO Black Book – A Guide to the Search Engine Optimization Industry's Secrets* - *http://www.amazon.com/dp/B00B7GIVSE*

- *Web 3.0 Startups – Online Marketing Strategies for Launching & Promoting any Business on the Web* - *http://www.amazon.com/dp/B00BYZB68U*

- *Viral – How to Spread your Ideas like a Virus* - *http://www.amazon.com/dp/B00C4G7EIE*

- *How Not to Give Up – A Motivational & Inspirational Guide to Goal Setting and Achieving your Dreams* - *http://www.amazon.com/dp/B00BSB02KI*

- *Kindle Self Publishing Gold – Unlocking the Secrets of How to Make Money Online with Kindle eBooks* - *http://www.amazon.com/dp/B00BQJB5QM*

- *Kindle Marketing Ninja Guide – Killer Marketing Strategies for Kindle Book Marketing Success* - *http://www.amazon.com/dp/B00BLR40FC*

SEO SIMPLIFIED – LEARN SEARCH ENGINE OPTIMIZATION
STRATEGIES AND PRINCIPLES FOR BEGINNERS

APPENDIX
SEO TERMINOLOGY

Aged Domains – An aged domain is a domain that has been in indexed by Google at least two or more years ago and it's a critical component of any successful SEO campaign. Google penalizes new domain names, making it very difficult to rank any keywords at the #1 position or even on the first page of search results for that matter in the beginning. Purchasing or having an aged domain will be one of the critical factors in your success for ranking a site high for any given keyword.

ALT tags – Also known as alternative tags, these are the tags that appear within the HTML <img> tags that present the alternate data to the search engines to provide a description of what the image is. For optimal search engine rankings you should have at least one image ALT tag that correlates with your site or page's primary keyword.

Backlinking – Likely to be your biggest undertaking when it comes to SEO, backlinking is the effort involved with creating hyperlinks that link back to your Website.

Black-Hat SEO – Black-Hat SEO is a term used to describe a SEO tactics that are not compliant with Google's Webmaster Guidelines. Black-Hat SEO techniques are frowned upon by the search engine industry. Examples of Black-Hat SEO techniques are trying to hide keywords within HTML comment tags or trying to cloak pages.

Breadcrumb – A navigational aid used on Websites, breadcrumbs not only allow users to quickly jump through informational sections on the site, they also provide high SEO value by allowing the search engine spiders access to quickly navigate and spider through a site, indexing data faster and more efficiently.

Cloaking – This is a technique that delivers different content to the search engine spiders then it does to real human visitors. The cloaking technique is oftentimes used to mask the real content or change the real content of a page and make it appear differently to a search engine spider. This is considered a Black-Hat SEO technique and while it is sometimes used for legitimate purposes, it is oftentimes used to display pornographic material to real human visitors while only displaying non-pornographic material to a search engine spider.

CPC – Cost-per-click, or CPC, is a term used in online paid advertising to indicate click through percentages. The cost per click is calculated by diving the number of clicks with the total amount spent on the advertisement. For example, if you spent $100 on an ad and 200 clicks was received; the CPC would be $0.50 cents.

CSS – Cascading Style Sheets, also known as CSS, is a style sheet presentation markup language that is used to position elements, layouts, colors, fonts, images, and construct a Web page on the whole. While CSS is used primarily in styling HTML Web pages, it is also used to style XML and other documents.

Dofollow Links – Dofollow links are an attribute associated with an HTML hyperlink that tell a search engine to continue to link through to the site, disseminating some of the site's important link juice. These are very powerful types of links that work well when pointed to your site or to a link pyramid that leads to your site. When a search engine sees a Dofollow link they continue linking through to the site, passing part of the SEO link juice that would have been offered to that page had the link been a Nofollow link.

Duplicate Content – In the search engine world, content is king, but duplicate content is the court jester. Copying large chunks of content to your site is one of the biggest no-no's in the industry. The search engines will figure it out sooner or later and you will be demoted in the rankings. If you're going to do SEO right, make sure all the content is high-quality and unique content that's well researched.

Headings – HTML headings are blocks of code that are placed around certain words, styling and providing a certain level of prominence in the overall page structure. Heading tags range from <h1> through <h6>, however, in the modern SEO world the first three hold the most importance. Tags <h1> through <h3> should all contain the primary keyword spaced throughout the page with the <h1> and <h2> tags being above the Website fold.

Internal Link – Internal links are links from your page's content to another page or section on the same domain. Internal links are important when it comes to On-Site SEO.

Keyword – A keyword is a word or phrase that is used to optimize a Website or Webpage. Selecting keywords is one of the most important tasks in SEO work and selecting the right keywords in the outset can either make or break you. It's important to note that the keyword "Miami vacation" and "vacation Miami" will produce different search results, so the order and positioning of the words within the phrase is just as important.

Keyword Density – The keyword density is the number of times a keyword appears on a page in relation to the total number of words. Optimal keyword density ranges from 2% to 5% with anything considerably over 5% being construed as SPAM and anything considerably lower then 2% being construed as not keyword rich enough and thus less relevant. It's important when writing your content that your primary keyword is evenly distributed throughout the page, making sure that it appears in the first and last sentence of the content as well as evenly spaced throughout the balance of the words.

Keyword Stuffing – Keyword stuffing is the over usage of a keyword in content or meta keyword tags, something that used to be popular many years ago, but is now frowned upon as a Black-Hat SEO technique. Keyword stuffing is achieved in various different ways which include placing the phrase multiple times within the Meta tags while combined with other words in different combinations, applying the same color to the keywords as the background making them invisible, using the <noscript> tag, and using CSS z-positioning. All of these practices will get you demoted and sometimes de-indexed by search engines like Google.

Long Tail Keyword – A long tail keyword is a keyword that has a minimum of at least 3 words and any maximum number of words. Long tail keywords are used by marketers trying to target a specific niche, question or topic, which produce near similar results to a broader search term of lessor keywords but may have higher competition. Long tail keywords are a great way to rank at the top of search engine results for terms that may otherwise be more difficult to rank for.

Link Bait – Link Bait refers to content that is created in order to garner as many links to it as possible. Since backlinks are one of the primary drivers of SERP positioning, many SEO efforts include the creation of content with the primary goal to get as many links back to that content as possible.

Link Farm – A link farm is a group of sites that all hyperlink to one another, back and forth in an oscillating fashion. While link farms used to be advantageous, they don't have large relevancy today since the two-way links make it confusing for search engines to determine which site is the vendor and which is the promoting site.

Link Juice – This is the SEO linking power of a page and usually refers to the combined sum of the link power of all the pages linking into it. You'll hear the term link juice referenced when quantifying the power of a certain link or a page that those links lead to.

Link Pyramid – A Link Pyramid is a very powerful form of Off-Site SEO backlinking that involves the creation of a linking structure that is extremely powerful. Think of the strength in physical form that a real pyramid has and how the transference of force is physically supported by the structure itself and how that has stood the test of time. Link Pyramids generally have three tiers: a bottom tier with low level links, a middle with medium level links, and a top level with high level EDU, GOV or other authority links. The bottom links link to the middle, the middle links link to the top, and the top links link to your site.

Link Sculpting – When you implement attributes to links to affect their behavior in how search engines interpret them, you're engaging in link sculpting. The most common form of link sculpting is using the Nofollow or Dofollow link sculpting forms. The Nofollow links tell a search engine not to follow a link, thus leaving the link juice on the page, while a Dofollow link tells a search engine to continue on to follow that link thus disseminating the link juice to the next page.

Link Wheel – A Link Wheel is a form of linking that links one site to another while also linking back to your site as well. The links flow in a sort of wheel format with the spokes being links back to your site in the center. When done correctly, a link wheel can be a powerful form of SEO boost for your Website and the most effective forms of link wheels are organically fashioned ones that utilize social media platforms as their linking mediums.

Meta Keywords – Meta keywords are part of a set of Meta Tags that appear in the header of Websites. Meta keywords used to be prominently used in search engine rankings but have no interpreted value of importance today. Instead of using meta keywords, search algorithms now use other tags such as heading tags, site content, keyword density and backlinking keywords to determine search engine rankings.

Meta Description – The meta description tag is one of the meta tags that are still used by search engines to display search results. This along with the title tag is used to display the name and description of the link on SERPs to the user searching for information.

Nofollow Links – Search engines spider the Web looking for information and in turn ranking the relevance of sites in its indexes. Nofollow links are an HTML attribute associated with hyper links that tell a search engine to not follow the link, stopping the search engine's traffic at that page, almost like a dead end. Nofollow links are optimal when it comes to making sure that your own page is optimized to the highest level possible by not allowing the link juice to pass through it.

Off-Site SEO – Off-Site SEO are the methods and practices of performing SEO work that happen away from the site itself. Off-Site SEO mainly involves the use of heavy backlinking, social media shares, authority site content creation (i.e. squidoo.com, youtube.com, etc.), article spinning, and so on. Off-Site SEO is a very labor-intensive part of the SEO trade.

On-Site SEO – Any work that is done on the Website to increase the effectiveness of its SEO is considered On-Site SEO. This includes any HTML work, content creation, internal linking, setup, keyword distribution, and other related efforts.

Page Title – The HTML page title is the descriptive site title detail that resides within the page's <title> tags. This information is displayed by the search engines and is used in ranking the site on the SERPs. A good page title tag should be descriptive but not superfluous and should accomplish its goal in around 70 characters (the cut off point for most SERPs) with the use of the primary keyword.

Pinging – Pinging is a technique that notifies the search engines to go out and seek data from a URL. This is required because a lot of the link building that is done happens on low, or no page rank sites that do not get visited often or at all by the search engines. When a search engine is pinged to go out and index a URL you can be certain that the hyperlink to your site or to another link in a link pyramid that's pointing to your site, will be found and indexed.

Panda – The Google Panda is a change in the algorithm for Google's search results that was released in February of 2011. The effects of Panda were to demote low quality sites and promote sites with high quality well researched information. The effects of this release were widespread, making huge shifts in positioning on SERPs forcing some businesses to lose large volumes of search traffic while others were able to gain it.

Page Rank – One of the most important descriptors of a Web page, the page rank is a Web page's rank in relevancy on the Internet, ranging from 0 to 10. Sites like Facebook, Twitter, and Google's home page achieve Page ranks of 9 and 10, while lower trafficked sites have lesser page ranks.

Penguin – The Google Penguin was one of the latest

major updates released to Google's algorithm on April 24th, 2012, that began to demote visibility of listings on SERPs that violated Google's Webmaster guidelines and employed Black-Hat SEO tactics such as cloaking, keyword stuffing, and the creation of duplicate content.

PPC - Pay-per-click advertising, or PPC, is a form of paid search engine advertising that marketers use to get their message out to the masses on a large scale very quickly. PPC ads show up on the right side of SERPs and are now also being implemented on Facebook, YouTube videos, and more recently on sites like Twitter.

PPV – Pay per view ads, or PPV, is a type of advertising that is utilized by marketers to distribute ads to a user base that has expressly agreed to receive those ads. An example of this is free software downloads or online services such as Pandora that use PPV ads to display advertisements on a periodic basis while providing a free service.

Referrer String – Referrer strings are used in affiliate and Web marketing to pinpoint campaigns and where a lead or referral came from. This is important to some marketers running paid advertisements to be able to gauge the successes of their various efforts throughout the Web. Web programming dictates that after the Web page name, a question mark can indicate the start of any variables that may be appended to a URL, thus resulting in a Referrer String.

Robots.txt – This is a file that resides in the root directory of your Website, that provides instructions to search engines on any folders, or files that it shouldn't index. Most people don't want search engines seeing all files on their sites such as administration files, or other files that contain sensitive information.

RSS Feed – A Rich Site Summary (RSS) feed is a standardized format that allows for the automatic update and syndication of content on sites that have frequent changes and entries such as blogs and other news sites. The RSS feed format provides a standard in formatting that allows ease of redistribution of either full or summarized data, metadata and publishing information.

Sandbox – Google Sandbox Effect is an effect that happens when a newly formed domain name's link juice is not fully weighted due to filtering from Google in order to prevent SPAMMERS from reaching the first page in SERPs by registering multiple domain names quickly and actively promoting them.

Search Algorithm – A formula devised by brilliant minds that weighs and takes multiple factors into account when reaching a determination for search result page ranking. The Google search algorithm combines many factors including the aged domain factor, Website link popularity, On-Site SEO elements, and Off-Site SEO elements. No one outside of Google knows the exact current algorithm and the total weight of each of the factors that are taken into account or precisely how they impact search results but there are very good guidelines available.

SEM – SEM is the business of search engine marketing, the industry that search engine optimization specialists fall under. SEM is used to refer to not only SEO efforts but also paid search engine marketing efforts as well.

SERP – Search Engine Ranking Pages, also known as SERPs, are the end listing results pages of queries to search engines. SERPs will generally include a title and brief description of each listing related to the keywords searched along with a link to that content. In SEO the goal is to dominate the first page of SERPs.

Sitemap – A sitemap is a page that's created to aid browsers in crawling a site. A sitemap provides a hierarchical link structure of pages on a Website that are accessible and permissible to be crawled.

Social Media – Social media is a term that refers to the types of sites that have increased in popularity in the past several years that base themselves on end user interactions in a social and collaborative format. Examples of such popular sites are Facebook, Google Plus, and Twitter.

Spider – A Spider is a Web-robot that's instructed to go out and crawl the Internet for data used for the purposes of Website indexing and rankings. Google has multiple spiders that it sends out, some that are dedicated to deep-indexing the Web, others for more periodic updates to

Web content, and even others for algorithm adjustments such as the Google Panda and Google Penguin.

Website Fold – The Website fold is the section of the Website that is viewable to the natural eye prior to getting cut off by the browser and forcing a user to scroll. The Website fold will vary from screen resolution to screen resolution, however it's typically 600 to 850 pixels down from the top of the browser.

White-Hat SEO – White-Hat SEO techniques are those that follow the rules and standards of the SEO world and also adhere to Google's Webmaster Guidelines. White-Hat SEO techniques, while more time intensive, offer the largest long-term gains for your Website's ranking on SERPs. These techniques include quality content creation, proper On-Site SEO configuration, and organically looking Off-Site SEO linking.